A Weekend in Pyongyang, North Korea

평양에서의 휴일

For Smaranda and Maria

스마란다와 마리아에게 바친다

For the photos of this album the author was awarded the International Photography Awards,
"Editorial Non-pro" category, and was nominated for "Discovery of the Year", Lucie Awards 2012.

이 화보의 사진들은 국제사진상 '비전문 에디터 부문'에서 수상했으며, 2012년 루시상 '올해의 발견' 최종 후보작으로 선정되었다.

A Weekend in Pyongyang, North Korea

평양에서의 휴일

Adelin Petrisor

아델린 페트리쇼르

Hollym

A Weekend in Pyongyang, North Korea
평양에서의 휴일

Copyright © 2016
by Adelin Petrisor

First published in 2016
by Hollym International Corp., USA
Phone 908 353 1655   **Fax** 908 353 0255
http://www.hollym.com   **e-Mail** contact@hollym.com

 Hollym

Published simultaneously in Korea
by Hollym Corp., Publishers, Seoul, Korea
Phone +82 2 734 5087   **Fax** +82 2 730 5149
http://www.hollym.co.kr   **e-Mail** info@hollym.co.kr

ISBN: 978-1-56591-482-7
Library of Congress Control Number: 2016942947

Printed in Korea

Adelin Petrisor (born in 1975) is one of the most famous war reporters in Romania. He began his career in 1994 at the radio station 2M+. He worked at Tele 7ABC, TVR, Antena 1 and Realitatea TV. He is today a special correspondent for the Romanian public television. He made live transmissions from Iraq, Afghanistan, Lebanon, Israel, Algeria, Albania, Egypt, Libya and other war zones. During the American offensive in Iraq, in 2003, he was the only Romanian reporter broadcasting from Baghdad. He interviewed personalities such as Yasser Arafat, Ehud Barak, Benjamin Netanyahu, Valentino Rossi, the Ayatollah Mohammad Fadlallah, Jaap de Hoop Scheffer and others. In 2006, he made a reportage from inside the American prison in Guantanamo. In 2007, he published a photo album entitled 『War correspondent (Corespondent de razboi)』. In 2010, his book 『My Wars (Razboaiele mele)』 was published at Polirom Publishing House. The Association of Television Professionals in Romania awarded him five times, including the Grand Award in 2003, the Award for the Best Reportage in 2007 and the Award for Political Documentary in 2009.

아델린 페트리쇼르(1975년생)는 루마니아에서 가장 유명한 종군기자 중 한 사람이다. 1994년 2M+ 라디오 방송국에 입사해 Tele 7ABC, TVR, Antena 1, Realitatea TV 등에서 근무했으며, 현재 루마니아 국영 방송국 특파원으로 활동하고 있다. 이라크, 아프가니스탄, 레바논, 이스라엘, 알제리, 알바니아, 이집트, 리비아 등 전쟁이 일어난 수많은 지역에서 생방송을 하였다. 2003년 미군이 이라크를 공격했을 당시 바그다드에서 생방송을 한 유일한 루마니아 기자였다. 그는 야세르 아라파트, 에후드 바라크, 베냐민 네타냐후, 발렌티노 로시, 무하마드 파들라라흐 아야톨라, 야프 더호프 스헤퍼르와 같은 유명 인사들과 인터뷰를 하기도 했다. 2006년에는 미국 관타나모 수용소 르포 기사를 썼으며, 2007년에는 『전쟁 특파원』이라는 화보집을 냈다. 그리고 2010년 저서 『나의 전쟁』을 폴리롬 출판사에서 출간하였다. 루마니아 텔레비전 전문가 협회에서 2003년 최우수상, 2007년 최고의 보도상, 2009년 정치 다큐멘터리상 등 모두 다섯 차례 수상하였다.

Rescuing our imagination

Romanians thought that the fall of communism meant capitalism, but what it really meant was just television. We are living the era where television broadcasts everything, but says nothing. I find it useless to continue on this line, for what we [Romanians] had started as a teledemocracy ended up being a teledepression. We started from just four hours a day of television and ended up in the whirl of forty different cable channels. How were we supposed to know that there is nothing such as a teledemocracy? Like many other Romanians have experienced, once you cross over the border of sadness, there is no competence anymore. We now know that we dislike television, that it hurts us; therefore we have stopped watching it. We have no idea of what will follow.

There are however a few things that I do know. One of them made me write this introduction. For example, I know that the allied soldiers in Iraq and Afghanistan, and among them the Romanian soldiers as well, use to urinate inside a pipe stuck in the ground, when they are detached far away from their base camp. It is Adelin Petrisor who let us know this in one of his war reports. Is it just a detail? Of course, but could you come up with something better? Think about any other trifle that a talk show or any other TV show came up with and forced it into your neurons, so that it will stay forever in your memory until the end of times. There are so many of them that, while watching the Romanian TV shows, you somehow get a feeling of being just a small gold fish inside a water bowl, with all your memories being erased the second you move on to something else, presented as more important.

And the example with the pipe, "The Pipe Brief" as we could call it so that we could remember it better in the general lack of attention, is not a singular example of how Adelin does his job. He is one of those journalists who, the more they analyze the detail, the more interesting their news is and who, the further they go with their investigations the closer they bring us to the news.

Some months ago he was in a rush to help his fellow workers from TVR News with some hot-news-of-the-moment. The president, or the prime minister or some political party was leaving or was taking power, something like that. Anyhow, it was something that although seemed to shatter in pieces the world as we know it, ended up by leaving the world completely unchanged. During the recordings he suddenly whispered to me behind the cameras, despite the overwhelming atmosphere of the political moment: "I am going to go to North Korea! I keep dreaming about this for the last couple of years." It was a very profound moment, and I said to myself that, if one of the most beautiful definitions of what a sport reporter tries to do on a daily basis is "The sport is a fight for our imagination", then Adelin too fights for our power of imagination, by filming and discovering new stories, except that the people he films are usually wearing long pants.

This is what the present album about North Korea means. We find in it the future that we [Romanians] were too lucky to get to see. We soothe ourselves with the idea that no matter how bad it is for us to live our lives inside TV sets, it is far better than to live with no freedom. This album shows us page by page how a reporter that we know from the TV takes a bow in front of the deep core of his own job, a job that is nothing but a fight for our stories and for our imagination.

Catalin Tolontan

상상력을 구하다

루마니아 사람들은 공산주의가 몰락하자 자본주의 시대가 열릴 것으로 생각했다. 하지만 실제로는 텔레비전의 시대가 되었다. 우리는 알맹이 없이 모든 것이 텔레비전에서 방송되는 시대를 살고 있다. 이러한 사실을 더 이상 왈가왈부할 필요가 없다는 것을 나는 안다. 왜냐하면 우리가 '전자민주주의'로 생각했던 것이 결국 '전자우울증'이 돼버렸기 때문이다. 처음에는 하루에 네 시간만 방송하던 것이 이제는 40개의 케이블 채널에서 연이어 방송하고 있다. '전자민주주의'가 존재할 수 없다는 것을 그때 예상할 수 있었을까? 많은 루마니아 사람들이 경험했던 것처럼 슬픔이 극에 달하면 더 이상 도움이 되지 않는다. 우리는 텔레비전이 해로울 수 있다는 것을 알기에 이전만큼 좋아하지도 않고 많이 보지도 않는다. 그것이 어떤 결과를 가져올지는 아무도 모른다.

하지만 확실히 알고 있는 것이 몇 가지 있다. 그중 하나가 내가 이 서문을 쓰는 이유다. 예를 들어 보자. 우리는 루마니아 군인을 포함한 이라크와 아프가니스탄 주둔 연합군들이 소속 부대에서 멀리 떨어져 있을 때 땅에 꽂힌 파이프 안에 소변을 본다는 사실을 아델린 페트리쇼르의 전쟁 보도로 알게 되었다. 이런 것들이 너무 사소한 이야기라고 생각하는가? 그렇다면 당신은 이보다 더 나은 이야기를 들려줄 수 있는가? 토크쇼나 다른 텔레비전 쇼에 나왔던 수많은 하찮은 이야기들 중 당신 머릿속에서 지워지지 않은 채 평생 뉴런에 박혀 있을 만한 것이 있는지 생각해 보자. 어쩌면 당신은 텔레비전을 볼 때 어항 속 작은 금붕어가 된 느낌을 받을지도 모른다. 텔레비전 화면이 사라질 때마다 당신의 기억도 함께 사라진다.

파이프 이야기로 돌아가 보자. 기억하기 쉽게 일명 '파이프 사건'이라고 부르는 이 이야기는 아델린 페트리쇼르가 하는 일을 보여 주는 좋은 예이다. 뉴스는 자세히 파고들면 들수록 더 흥미로워지고, 조사를 많이 하면 할수록 더 생생하게 다가온다. 그는 그렇게 할 수 있는 기자이다.

몇 달 전 아델린은 특보 뉴스 때문에 TVR 뉴스 동료들을 도와주느라 정신이 없었다. 그 특보는 대통령이나 국무총리, 혹은 어떤 정당이 실각하거나 권력을 얻었다는 등의 뉴스였다. 당시에는 세상이 뒤집힐 만한 중대 사건이라고 생각했지만, 되짚어 보면 별것 아닌 사건이었다. 아무튼 당시 정치적 사건의 중대성에도 불구하고 그는 방송 중인 카메라 뒤로 와서 나에게 속삭였다. "나 이번에 북한에 간다! 지난 몇 년 동안 꿈꿔 왔던 일이야." 그것은 정말 뜻깊은 순간이었다. 만약 스포츠 기자가 매일 하는 일을 '사람들의 상상력을 위한 싸움'이라고 아름답게 정의한다면, 아델린도 새로운 이야기를 찾아내고 그것을 카메라에 담으면서 비슷한 싸움을 하고 있다고 할 수 있다. 다만 스포츠 기자와 달리 아델린이 촬영하는 사람들은 대부분 긴 바지를 입고 있을 뿐이다.

이 책에서 우리는 루마니아 사람들이 조금만 운이 나빴다면 겪게 되었을지도 모르는 미래를 볼 수 있다. 북한에 대한 이 화보는 바로 그런 의미를 갖는다. 아무리 텔레비전 속에 갇혀 사는 것이 나쁘다고 할지라도 자유 없이 사는 것보다는 훨씬 낫다는 사실에 위안을 얻을 수도 있다. 기자라는 직업은 우리의 상상력을 위해 많은 이야기를 들려주고자 싸우는 일이다. 우리는 아델린이 기자로서 자신의 본분에 충실하기 위해 얼마나 노력했는지 사진 속에서 엿볼 수 있다.

커틸린 톨론탄

North Korea:
The Country as Concentration Camp

I dreamed since childhood to visit the country of Kim Il-sung, the one most reliable friend of Nicolae Ceausescu, the leader of socialist Romania. I had been told that North Korean students learn at school that their leader has superhuman powers: he was bringing the rain, was talking with the cranes, and at his death, even the swallows mourned him. I don't believe there is a single journalist that wouldn't want to find out what's happening in the most isolated country in the world.

For six years prior to my visit I had been corresponding and had meetings with the officials of the North Korean embassy in Bucharest. It had been meant to be a complicated affair. Closeted inside the embassy located in an exclusive area of the Romanian capital city, the North Korean officials avoid talking to journalists. I remember that on my first meeting with them, I hadn't even been received inside the garden surrounding the building. An official came outside on the sidewalk, looked right and left and closed the heavy gate with a remote control, fearful as if I was about to run inside their embassy and request asylum.

I handed him over the visa request; he took it without saying a word and disappeared again behind the door. Years have passed without any answer. I followed up with hundreds of phone calls, emails and faxes, until one day a new ambassador, formerly accredited to France, came to Bucharest. He was a pleasant person and open-minded, if we were to consider the North Korean standard. He was fluent in both English and French and he invited me over a couple of times, when we drank coffee, smoked cigars and discussed about North Korea. Two years after our first meeting, he finally gave me the good news: I was allowed to travel to Pyongyang as an accredited foreign journalist, permission usually very hard to obtain.

My first contact with the country of Kim was, as I had expected, very tough. One cannot be but moved by the shabby airport, by the general grey of the buildings, by the people all dressed up in dull colors who, the moment they realize you are watching them, fearfully turn their heads and almost start running in the opposite direction. In Pyongyang I have seen things that had marked my childhood spent in the communist Romania: large queues outside shops, huge boulevards almost deserted by people and cars, absurdly immense buildings. At every intersection large speakers were shouting motivational speeches and the huge banners were being filled just with communist propaganda. The leader is everywhere, except in the food, that is never sufficient. The Orwellian landscape made me shiver and I thought that this is how Romania would have looked like, had there been no revolution in December 1989. I suddenly remembered that people don't learn from their mistakes and from what history teaches us. Seeing what is happening for ages in North Korea and bearing into my mind pieces of painful memories from the time of Romanian communism, I can just hope that, at least this time, we have been learning our lessons.

Adelin Petrisor

북한, 수용소가 된 나라

나는 어렸을 적부터 김일성의 나라에 가보는 것이 꿈이었다. 그는 공산주의 시절 루마니아 지도자였던 니콜라에 차우셰스쿠의 가장 믿을 만한 친구였다. 북한 학생들은 학교에서 김일성의 초인적 능력에 대해서 배운다고 들었다. 그가 비를 몰고 오고, 학과도 대화할 수 있다는 것이다. 그가 죽었을 때에는 제비들마저 슬프게 울었다고 했다. 기자치고 세상에서 가장 고립된 그 나라에서 무슨 일이 벌어지는지 알고 싶지 않은 기자는 없을 거라 생각한다.

나는 북한에 가기 6년 전부터 부쿠레슈티에 있는 북한대사관 관리들과 자주 연락을 주고받았으며 만나기도 했다. 북한을 방문하는 것은 그만큼 복잡한 문제였다. 북한 관리들은 루마니아 수도의 배타적 지역에 위치한 북한대사관에 들어앉아 기자들과의 만남을 꺼렸다. 그들을 처음 만났을 때 건물을 둘러싸고 있는 정원에조차 들어가지 못했다. 대신 관리 한 명이 밖에 있는 인도로 나왔다. 그는 나오면서도 좌우를 조심스럽게 살피며 마치 내가 대사관으로 뛰어들어가 망명 신청이라도 할까 봐 두려운 듯 육중한 문을 리모컨으로 잠갔다.

나는 그에게 비자 신청서를 내밀었다. 그는 아무 말 없이 서류를 받아 다시 문 뒤로 사라졌다. 그 뒤로 몇 년이 지나도록 아무 연락이 없었다. 물론 나는 수백 번 전화를 걸었고, 이메일과 팩스를 보냈다. 그러던 어느 날, 프랑스에서 근무하던 북한 대사가 부쿠레슈티로 부임해 왔다. 그는 유쾌한 사람이었으며, 북한 사람치고는 꽤나 개방적인 사고를 가지고 있었다. 그는 영어와 불어를 유창하게 했으며, 나를 여러 번 초대하여 함께 커피도 마시고, 시가도 피우며, 북한에 대한 이야기를 나누었다. 그렇게 2년이 지난 어느 날, 그는 마침내 좋은 소식을 들려주었다. 외국 기자로서 얻기 매우 어려운 평양 방문 허가가 났다는 것이다.

북한과의 첫 만남은 예상했던 대로 힘들었다. 허름한 공항, 사방의 회색 빌딩들, 칙칙한 색깔의 옷을 입고 남의 시선을 느끼면 무섭게 고개를 돌려 버리고 반대 방향으로 거의 뛰다시피 가는 사람들을 보면 감상에 젖을 수밖에 없었다. 어린 시절 루마니아에서 경험했던 것들을 평양에서도 보았다. 상점 밖에까지 길게 줄을 선 사람들, 사람이나 차가 거의 다니지 않는 대로, 터무니없이 큰 빌딩들. 사거리마다 커다란 확성기에서는 자극적인 연설들이 쏟아져 나왔고, 대형 현수막들은 공산주의 선전으로 가득 차 있었다. 그들의 지도자는 식료품을 제외한 모든 곳에 있었다. 음식은 늘 모자랐다. 조지 오웰의 소설 같은 분위기를 볼 때마다 전율이 느껴졌다. 루마니아에서 1989년 12월 혁명이 일어나지 않았더라면 그와 같았을 것이라는 생각이 들었다. 사람들은 자신의 실수나 역사가 가르쳐 주는 것들을 배우려 하지 않는다는 사실이 불현듯 떠올랐다. 루마니아 공산주의 시대의 아픈 기억을 간직하고 있는 우리가 지금 북한에서 일어나고 있는 일들을 보고, 적어도 이번만큼은 교훈을 얻길 희망할 수밖에 없다.

아델린 페트리쇼르

I. PYONGYANG : PEOPLE AND PLACES
I. 평양 : 사람과 장소

An old aircraft (model IL 62) of the North Korean airline company, Air Koryo, on the ramp at Beijing Capital International Airport
베이징 국제공항에 있는 고려항공의 오래된 비행기. 기종은 IL 62

◄ North Korean journalists and tour guides waiting for the foreign media representatives to arrive at Pyongyang Sunan International Airport
평양 순안국제공항에서 외신 기자들을 기다리고 있는 북한 기자와 가이드들

▲ The car of a North Korean Army General and busses waiting for journalists in the parking lot of the airport
공항 주차장에 대기 중인 어느 군 장성의 자동차와 외신 기자들을 위한 버스

▲ Convenience store inside Pyongyang Sunan International Airport 평양 순안국제공항 안에 있는 상점
▼ Two border guards at Pyongyang Sunan International Airport 평양 순안국제공항에서 본 두 명의 국경경비대원

1
2
3
▶

1. North Korean soldiers painting the edge of the sidewalk on the road linking the airport to the city
   공항과 도시를 잇는 도로의 보도 가장자리를 페인트칠 하고 있는 북한 군인들

2. North Korean soldier riding a bike on the road between the airport and Pyongyang
   공항과 평양 사이 도로를 자전거로 달리는 북한 군인

3. A public library on the road to Pyongyang
   평양으로 가는 길에 있는 도서관

◀ North Korean photographer preparing to take photos of his foreign colleagues
외국 손님들을 찍기 위해 준비하고 있는 북한 사진기자

North Korean propaganda billboards along boulevards in Pyongyang ▶
평양 길거리에서 볼 수 있는 북한 선전물

◀ Modern building near the entry in Pyongyang
평양 근교에 위치한 현대식 건물

▲ Block of apartments on the road linking the airport to the capital city
공항과 도심을 잇는 도로 옆에 있는 아파트 단지

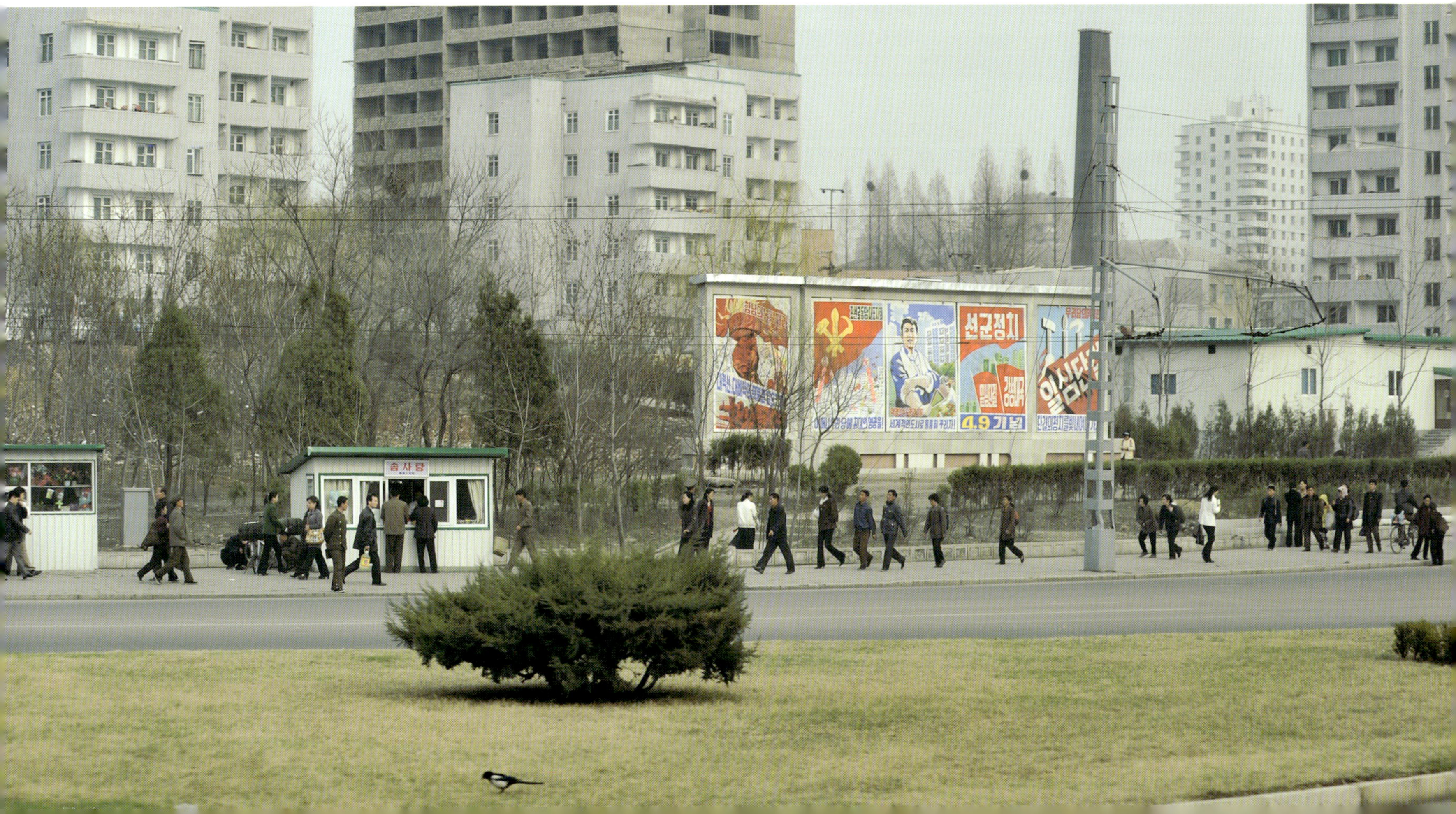

▲ Group of North Koreans coming out of the subway station
지하철역에서 나오고 있는 북한 사람들

1
2

▶

1. One of the major crossroads in Pyongyang
   평양의 주요 교차로 중 하나

2. Traffic on one of the biggest avenues in Pyongyang
   평양에서 가장 큰 도로 중 한 곳의 통행량

◀ Woman carrying a bundle on the road linking the airport to the capital
짐을 머리에 이고 도심과 공항을 잇는 길을 걸어가는 여성

▲ One of the busiest boulevards in Pyongyang
평양의 번화가 중 하나

▲ North Korean men repairing a Volga car 볼가 자동차를 수리 중인 북한 남자들
▼ Female police officer directing traffic in one of the busiest crossroads in the city 붐비는 사거리에서 교통정리를 하는 여경

One of the busiest boulevards in North Korea

북한에서 가장 붐비는 거리 중 하나

Yanggakdo Hotel, 48-Story, where are accommodating ▶
the few foreign tourists who visit North Korea
외국인 방문객에게 숙소로 제공하는 48층짜리 양각도국제호텔

◀ Pyongyang Central Station
평양역

▲ North Koreans crossing the street on a busy avenue in Pyongyang
평양 번화가의 횡단보도를 건너는 북한 사람들

▲ ▶ Sunset and sunrise over Pyongyang, as seen from the Yanggakdo Hotel
양각도국제호텔에서 바라본 평양의 일몰과 일출

1
2
3

◄

1. Bridge across the Taedong River, in Pyongyang
   평양의 대동강을 가로지르는 대교

2. Sunset in Pyongyang, as seen from the Yanggakdo Hotel
   양각도국제호텔에서 바라본 평양의 저녁놀

3. The night skyline of downtown Pyongyang,
   as seen from the main entrance in the Yanggakdo Hotel
   양각도국제호텔 입구에서 바라본 평양 시내의 야경

Parking lot of Yanggakdo Hotel, early in the morning ▶
이른 아침, 양각도국제호텔의 주차장

Dredging barges on the Taedong River ▶
대동강 준설 작업을 하고 있는 바지선

29

▲ Misty Pyongyang, as seen from the Yanggakdo Hotel 양각도국제호텔에서 바라본 안개 낀 평양 시내

▲ A newly-built neighborhood in the capital city of North Korea 평양의 신축 단지

▼ Yanggakdo Stadium in Pyongyang, on a misty morning 안개 낀 아침, 평양의 양각도 축구경기장

◄▲ Juche Tower, a landmark of Pyongyang
평양의 랜드마크, 주체탑

▲ Monument to the Party Founding, downtown Pyongyang
평양 시내의 노동당 창건 기념탑

◀ The Ryugyong Hotel, iconic building, whose failed construction began in 1987. The building was never completed.

평양의 상징적 건물로 1987년에 착공했으나 아직도 준공되지 않은 류경호텔

▲ Fountain in downtown Pyongyang 평양 시내의 분수

▼ New buildings in Pyongyang versus the image of an old and dirty neighborhood 평양의 새 건물들과 대조되는 낡고 지저분한 지역의 모습

The skyline of downtown Pyongyang
평양 시내의 스카이라인

▲ Skyscrapers in Pyongyang; although beautifully illuminated, these buildings are uninhabited and are meant only to impress the few foreign tourists
평양의 고층 건물들. 조명이 아름답게 빛나고 있지만 이 건물들에는 사람이 살지 않는다. 오로지 소수의 외국인 관광객들에게 깊은 인상을 남기기 위한 것이다.

◀ New buildings in Pyongyang
평양의 신축 건물들

Pyongyang Central Station at sunset ▶
해질녘의 평양역

▲ Bus depot in Pyongyang at sunset 평양의 한 버스 차고지에 비친 저녁놀

▼ North Korean man fishing on the river flowing through Pyongyang 평양에 흐르는 강에서 낚시를 하고 있는 북한 남자

▶ North Korean workers
북한 노동자들

▼ Workers on a construction site during the morning assembly
조례를 하고 있는 공사장 노동자들

▲ North Korean flag 인공기

1	2
	3

Drivers of North Korean officials
북한 관리들의 개인 운전기사들

▲ Buses parked in front of Yanggakdo Hotel,
accommodating only foreign tourists
양각도국제호텔 앞에 주차되어 있는 외국인 관광객
전용 버스

◄▲ Workers during the final preparations for the celebration of the 100th anniversary of the birth of Kim Il-sung

김일성 탄생 100주년 기념 행사 준비를 마무리하고 있는 노동자들

◀▼▶
Workers arranging the flowers before the massive celebrations honoring the birth of Kim Il-sung
김일성 탄생을 기념하는 대규모 행사에 앞서 꽃밭을 다듬고 있는 노동자들

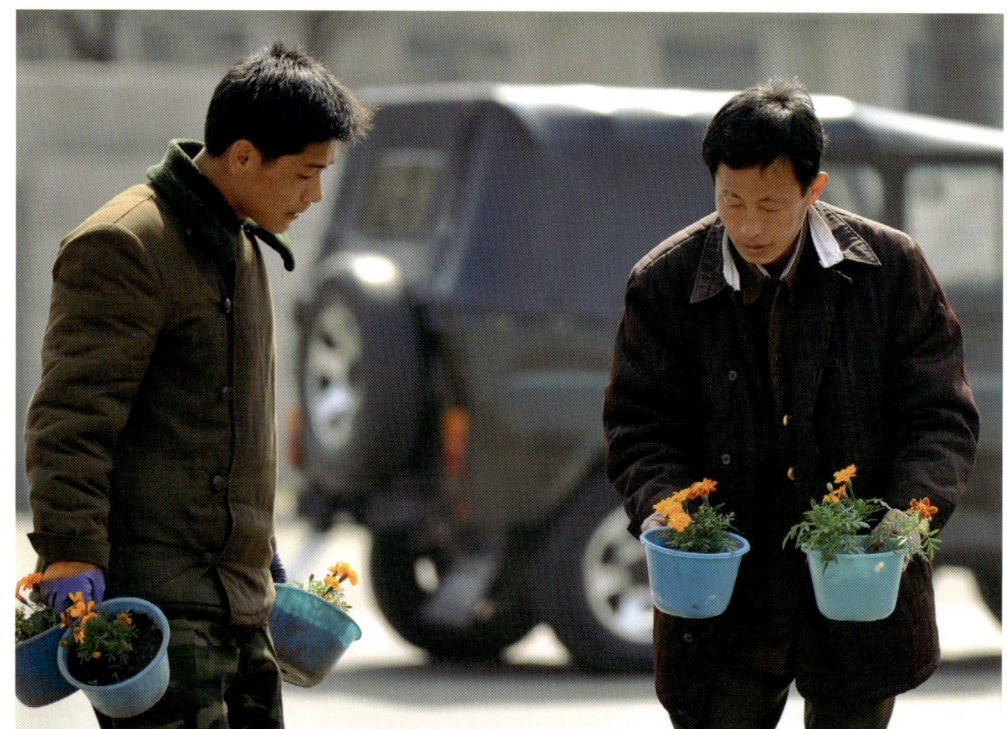

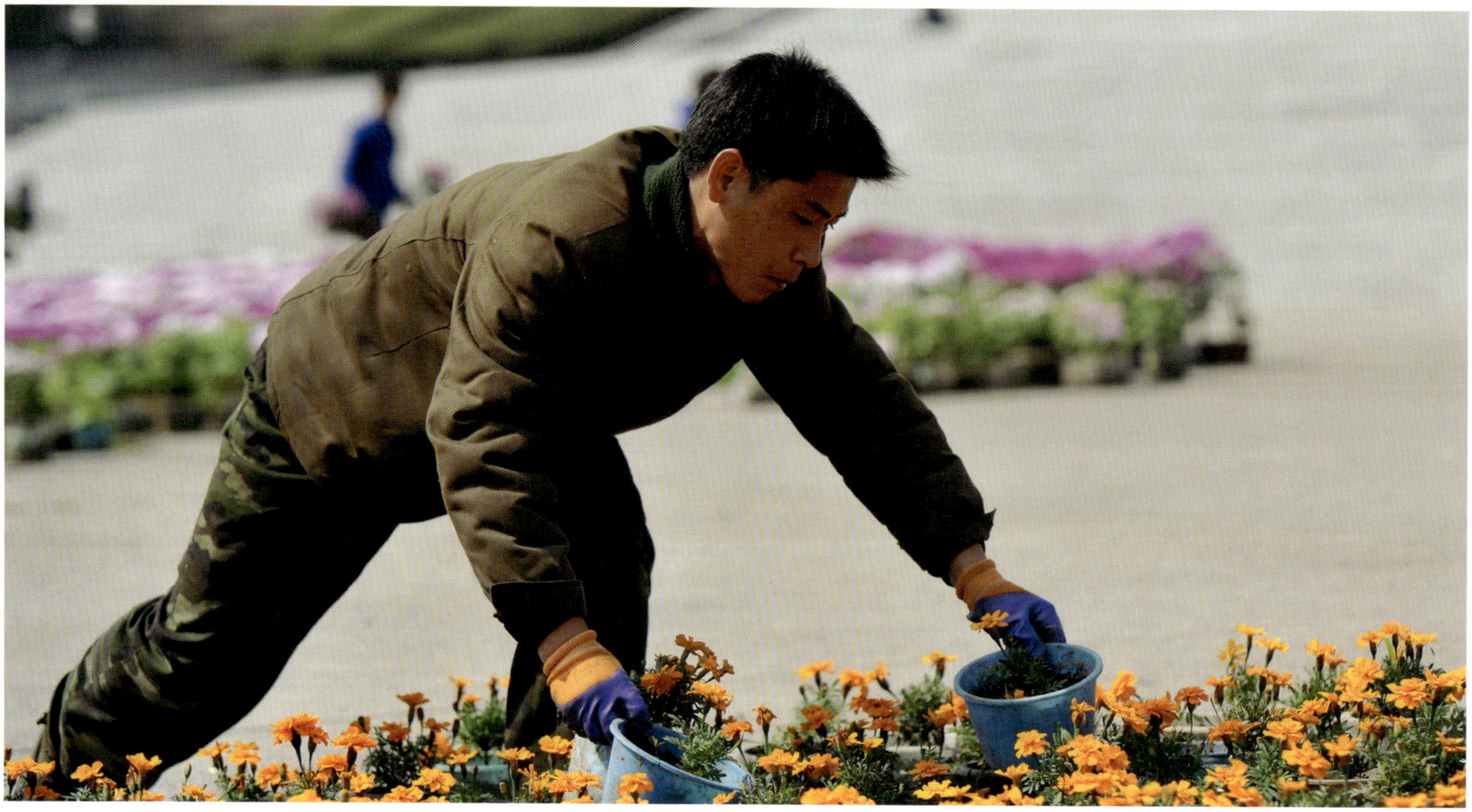

▲▼ Soldiers preparing the festivities and marching through downtown Pyongyang
행사를 준비하며 평양 시내를 행진하고 있는 군인들

Policeman guarding the workers who arrange the public spaces ▶

공공 장소를 정비하는 노동자를 지켜보는 경찰관

▲ Soldiers with rags wiping the water on a boulevard in central Pyongyang, before a visit of Kim Jong-un

김정은의 현장 방문을 앞두고 평양 중심가 큰길을 물걸레로 청소하고 있는 북한 군인들

◀ North Korean workers
북한 노동자들

▲ Girls from The Red Youth Guard walking through Pyongyang
평양 시내를 걷고 있는 붉은청년근위대 여성들

North Korean students ▶
북한 대학생들

▲ Girls from the Young Pioneer Corps walking
이동 중인 조선소년단 소녀들

51

◀ An old North Korean subway train
오래된 북한 전동차

▲ Yonggwang station of Pyongyang Metro
평양 지하철 '영광역'

54

People coming out of the subway station ▶
and heading towards the parade
지하철역에서 나와 행사장으로 가는 사람들

▲ People reading the newspaper displayed at the subway station
지하철역에 붙은 신문을 읽고 있는 사람들

◀▼ Mothers and children in downtown Pyongyang
평양 시내에서 본 어머니와 아이들

◀ North Korean child in a subway station
지하철역에서 만난 북한 어린이

▲◀ ▲ A walk through downtown
시내를 산책하는 사람들

▲▼ People waiting for the parade to start
행사가 시작되길 기다리는 사람들

▲▶ People resting during rehearsals for the parade
행사 연습이 진행되는 동안 앉아 쉬고 있는 사람들

◀ North Koreans bowing in front of the equestrian statues of Kim Il-sung and Kim Jong-il
김일성과 김정일의 기마상 앞에서 고개 숙여 절하는 북한 사람들

▲ Female police officers in front of an administrative building in Pyongyang 평양의 한 정부 기관 입구를 지키고 있는 여성 경찰관

▲ Children on a street in Pyongyang 평양 거리에서 만난 아이들

▲ The most coveted store in Pyongyang, the convenience store of the Yanggakdo Hotel, where one could find foreign liquors, local cigarettes, Russian bonbons and Chinese canned meat
평양에서 가장 인기 있는 양각도국제호텔의 편의점. 수입 양주, 북한산 담배, 러시아산 봉봉, 중국산 통조림 고기 등을 팔고 있다.

▲ A poster of the International Art Festival,
an event marking the 100th anniversary of the birth of Kim Il-sung
김일성 탄생 100주년을 기념하는 국제예술축제 포스터

▲ North Korean man dressed in uniform 인민복을 입은 북한 남자
▼ Traffic police officer in Pyongyang 평양의 교통경찰관

▲ Crowd at the front desk of the Yanggakdo Hotel 양각도국제호텔 프런트 앞의 사람들

▼ The only connection with the outside world: the telephones in the lobby of the Yanggakdo Hotel 외부 세계와의 유일한 연결 통로인 양각도국제호텔 로비의 전화기

▲▼
Photo shooting necessary for admission to the festivities
marking the 100ᵗʰ anniversary of the birth of Kim Il-sung
김일성 탄생 100주년 기념 행사에 입장하는 데 필요한 사진을
찍고 있다.

▲ The setting for a live transmission from the courtyard of the Yanggakdo Hotel 양각도국제호텔 앞 생방송을 위한 장치들

▼ NBC team preparing for a live broadcast from Pyongyang 평양 생방송을 준비하고 있는 NBC 촬영팀

▲ TVR (Romanian Television) cameraman Catalin Popescu in front of an art gallery in Pyongyang
평양의 한 미술관 앞 루마니아 방송국 TVR 카메라맨 커털린 포페스쿠

▼ The Press Center of the Yanggakdo Hotel 양각도국제호텔의 프레스센터

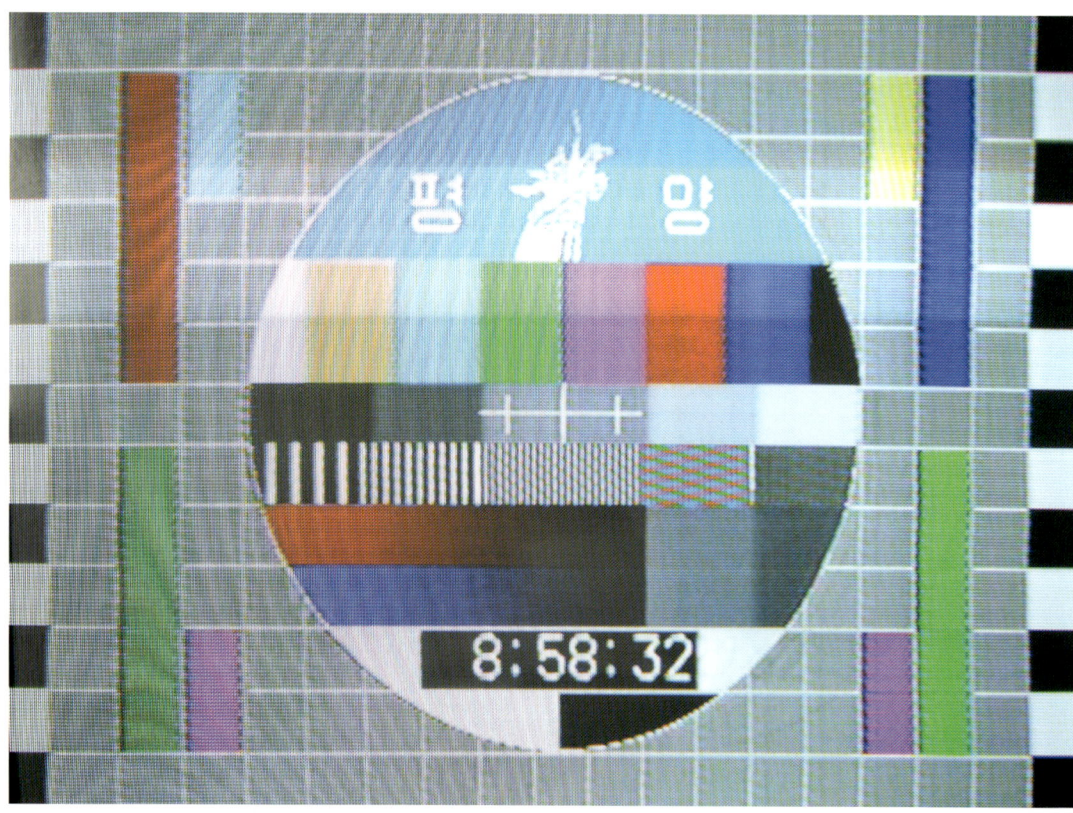

◀ The test pattern of the North Korean Television
right before the start of the broadcasting
방송 시작 직전 북한 텔레비전의 조정 화면

◀ Old radio set inside a hotel room
호텔 방 안의 낡은 라디오

▲ Taking a short break between two parades
행사 막간의 짧은 휴식 시간

II. THE ARMY AND THE SUPREME COMMANDER
II. 북한군과 그들의 최고사령관

A large propaganda poster in uptown Pyongyang, depicting the founder of the country, Kim Il-sung, together with the armed forces, workers and intellectuals
평양 외곽에 걸린 커다란 선전 벽보. 군인과 노동자, 지식인들이 북한 정권을 세운 김일성과 함께 그려져 있다.

▲ Quote of Kim Jong-il inside a public library from Pyongyang, placed above shelves of books with the works of the "beloved leaders"
평양 국립도서관 안에 '경애하는 지도자들'의 저서로 가득 채워져 있는 책꽂이와 그 위에 걸려 있는 김정일의 명언

◀ Soldiers in charge of security during a rally where the supreme leader Kim Jong-un was expected to attend
최고 지도자 김정은이 참석할 예정인 행사에서 안전을 담당한 군인들

▲ The statues of Kim Il-sung and Kim Jong-il, seconds after unveiling
김일성과 김정일 동상 제막식 직후의 모습

North Koreans bowing before the statues of Kim Il-sung and Kim Jong-il ▶
김일성과 김정일 동상에 절하고 있는 북한 사람들

▲▼▶
Civilians and soldiers,
waiting for a popular parade to start
행사가 시작되기를 기다리고 있는 일반인과 군인들

North Koreans applauding frantically after the ▶
unveiling of the two leader's statues
김일성과 김정일 동상 제막식 후
열광적으로 박수를 치고 있는 북한 사람들

Some participants at a popular parade
대중적 행사에 참가한 북한 사람들

▲ Kim Jong-un flanked by generals and prominent party members, during the ceremony of unveiling the statues of Kim Il-sung and Kim Jong-il

김일성과 김정일 동상 제막식에 참석한 김정은 양옆으로 도열한 장군들과 주요 노동당원들

◀▲▼
People gathered in the capital city to attend the unveiling of Kim Il-sung and Kim Jong-il's statues

김일성과 김정일 동상 제막식에 참여하기 위해 평양에 운집한 사람들

◀▶
Attendees at the unveiling of Kim Il-sung
and Kim Jong-il's statues
김일성과 김정일 동상 제막식 참가자들

▲ Tens of thousands of civilians and soldiers leaving downtown Pyongyang after a prodigious popular parade
엄청난 규모의 대중적 행사가 끝난 후, 평양 시내를 떠나는 수만 명의 일반인과 군인들

◄▲ North Koreans leaving downtown Pyongyang after the monumental parade
기념 행사가 끝난 후 평양 시내를 떠나는 북한 사람들

A giant portrait of Kim Il-sung on a building in downtown Pyongyang ▶
평양 시내 노동당 중앙당사에 걸려 있는 커다란 김일성 초상화

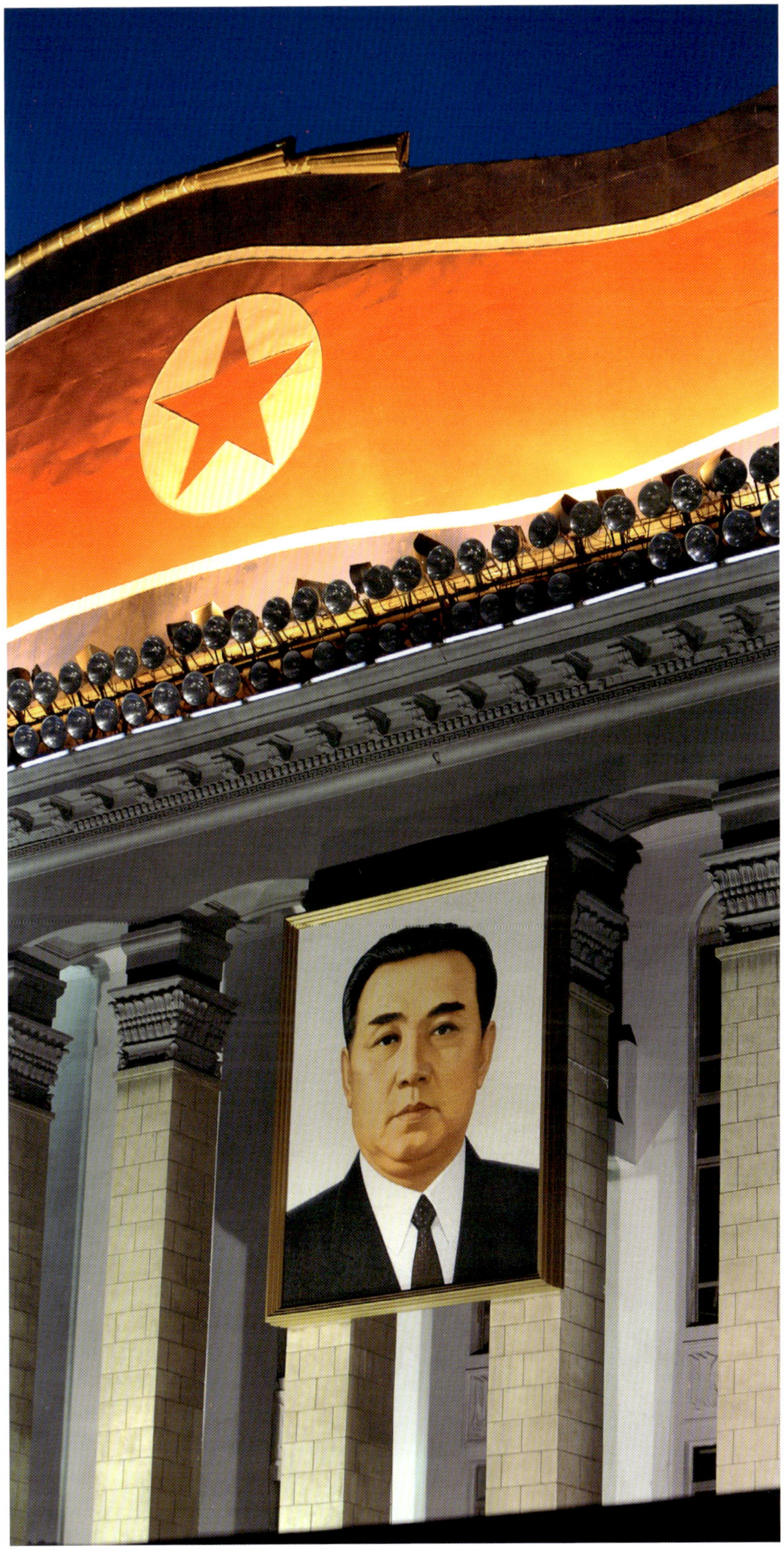

▲ Portraits of Kim Il-sung and Kim Jong-il in front of Pyongyang high-rises
평양의 고층 빌딩 앞에 설치된 김일성과 김정일의 초상화

Soldiers rushing towards the stadium where they are to meet their leader, Kim Jong-un
지도자 김정은을 맞이하기 위해 경기장으로 뛰어가는 군인들

▲ Soldiers rushing towards the stadium where they are to meet their leader, Kim Jong-un 지도자 김정은을 맞이하기 위해 경기장으로 뛰어가는 군인들

▼ A section of a stadium in Pyongyang, with soldiers waiting for the supreme commander 평양 경기장의 관람석에 앉아 최고사령관 김정은을 기다리는 군인들

▲ Military officer at a parade 열병식에 참석한 육군 장교

▲▼▶
Soldiers attending a large parade
대규모 행사에 참석한 군인들

Soldiers waiting for the arrival of Kim Jong-un
김정은이 도착하길 기다리는 군인들

▲▼
Cheers and applause at the sight of
the supreme commander, Kim Jong-un
최고사령관 김정은이 나타나자 터지는 환호와 박수갈채

Kim Jong-un flanked by generals and party members ▶
during a meeting with North Korean soldiers
장군들과 노동당원들 사이에 서서 북한군을 만난 김정은

▼ The grandstand of the stadium where the meeting between
Kim Jong-un and the soldiers took place
김정은과 군인들의 만남이 이루어진 경기장의 주석단

◄ A Japanese photographer attending a large scale parade in Pyongyang
평양에서 열린 대규모 행사에 참석한 일본인 사진작가

▲ Officer yawning during a speech at an official ceremony 공식 행사의 연설 도중 하품을 하고 있는 군인

▲▼ Soldiers sitting at attention while attending a large parade 대규모 행사에 참석하고 있는 내내 집중해서 앉아 있는 군인들

▼ ▼ ▶
Soldiers applauding and cheering during the meeting
with the supreme commander Kim Jong-un
최고사령관 김정은에게 박수와 환호를 보내는 군인들

▲ Rushed withdrawal from the stadium where the meeting with the supreme commander took place 최고사령관과의 만남 뒤 경기장을 빠져나가는 군인들

► An old camera used by the North Korean journalists to film the parade
북한 기자들이 행사를 촬영하는 데 사용한 낡은 카메라

▼ A North Korean television cameraman preparing to broadcast a huge military parade in Pyongyang
대규모 열병식 방송을 준비 중인 북한 방송국의 카메라맨

▲ The grandstand at the military parade celebrating the 100th anniversary of the birth of Kim Il-sung 김일성 탄생 100주년을 기념하는 열병식이 진행되는 주석단

▼ Soldiers preparing to parade in front of the grandstand 주석단 앞에서 행진을 준비하고 있는 군인들

▲ The parade opener 열병식의 선두
▼ North Korean Military Fanfare 북한 군악대

▲ Military fanfare opening the parade celebrating the 100ᵗʰ anniversary of the birth of Kim Il-sung 김일성 탄생 100주년을 기념하는 열병식의 시작을 알리는 군악대

▼ The North Korean Honor Guard escorting the flag 깃발을 들고 있는 북한 의장대

Soldier coming to attention ▶
for the raising of the flag
인공기가 게양되는 것을 지켜보고 있는 군인

▲ Flag rising on the mast 게양되고 있는 깃발

▼ Military cameraman filming the parade 열병식을 찍고 있는 카메라 담당 군인

▲▼ The commander of the parade, passing by the grandstand in a brand new limousine, a sharp contrast with the poverty of the North Korean people
북한 사람들의 궁핍한 삶과 극명하게 대비되는 최신식 리무진을 타고 주석단 앞을 지나고 있는 부대장

▲▼▶
Soldiers passing by the grandstand in perfect order and saluting the officials
당원들에게 경의를 표하며 절도 있게 주석단을 지나고 있는 군인들

▲ Parade rank of the Air Force 공군 행진 대열

◀▶
Parade rank of the Marines
해병대 행진 대열

▲ Parade rank of woman soldiers 여군 행진 대열

▲ Female officers saluting 거수경례하고 있는 여군

▲ Flag guard 깃발을 들고 행진하는 군인들

| 1 |
| 2 |
| 3 |

▶

1-2. Parade ranks of woman from the Army
여군 행진 대열

3. North Korean Navy's women sailors
북한 해군의 여성 대원

113

◄
Tankers
탱크 운전기사들

◄▶
Soldiers on parade passing by the grandstand
주석단 앞을 지나가는 군인들

Soldiers armed with AG-7 rocket launchers
AG-7 로켓 발사기로 무장한 군인들

▲ The Cavalry passing by the grandstand 주석단 앞을 지나는 기병들
▼ Women medical corps marching smartly 힘차게 행진하고 있는 여성 의무대

◀ Commander of the Cavalry leads parade
행진을 이끌고 있는 기병대장

▲▼◄►
Soldiers boarded in trucks
트럭에 탄 군인들

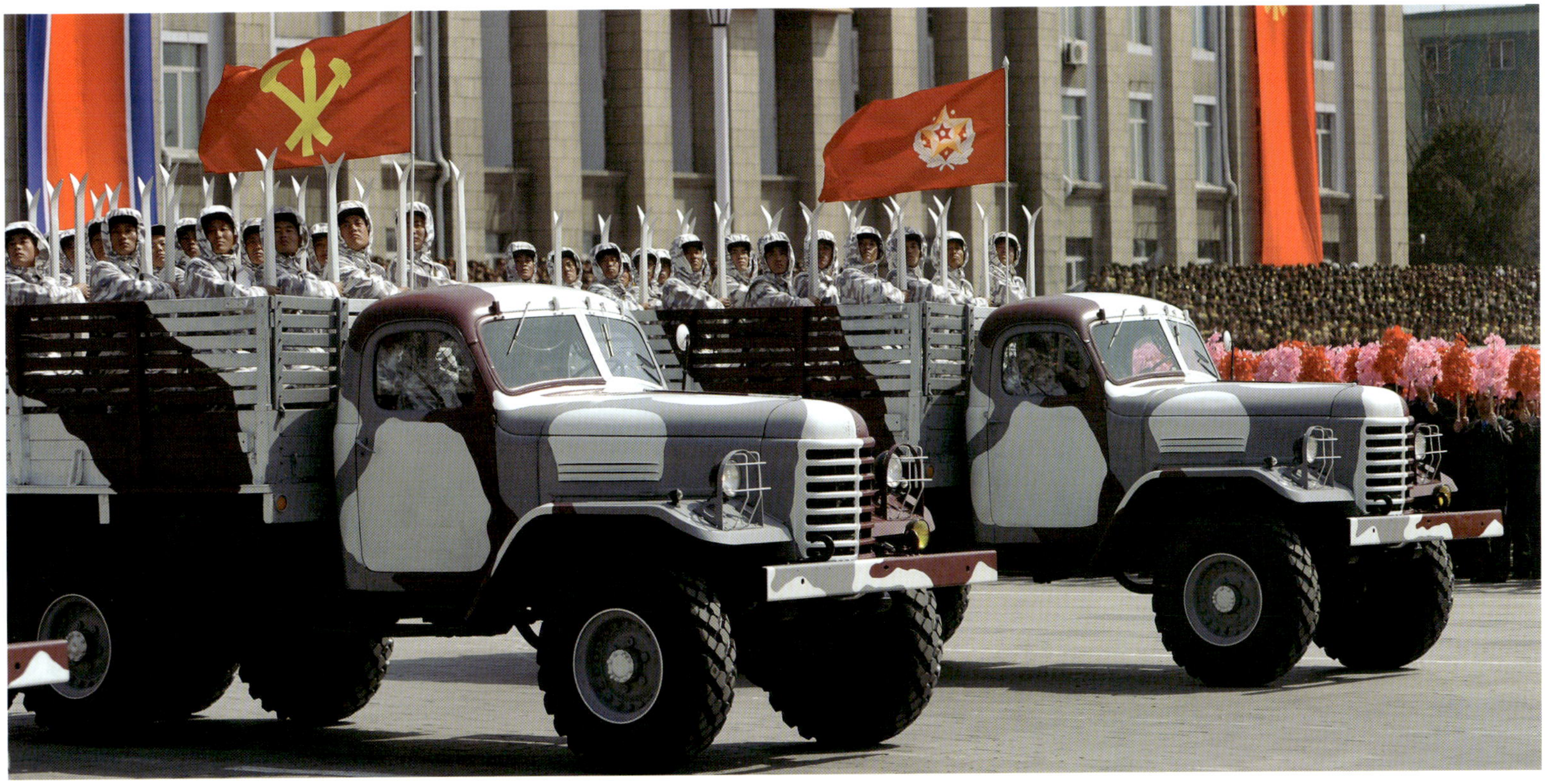

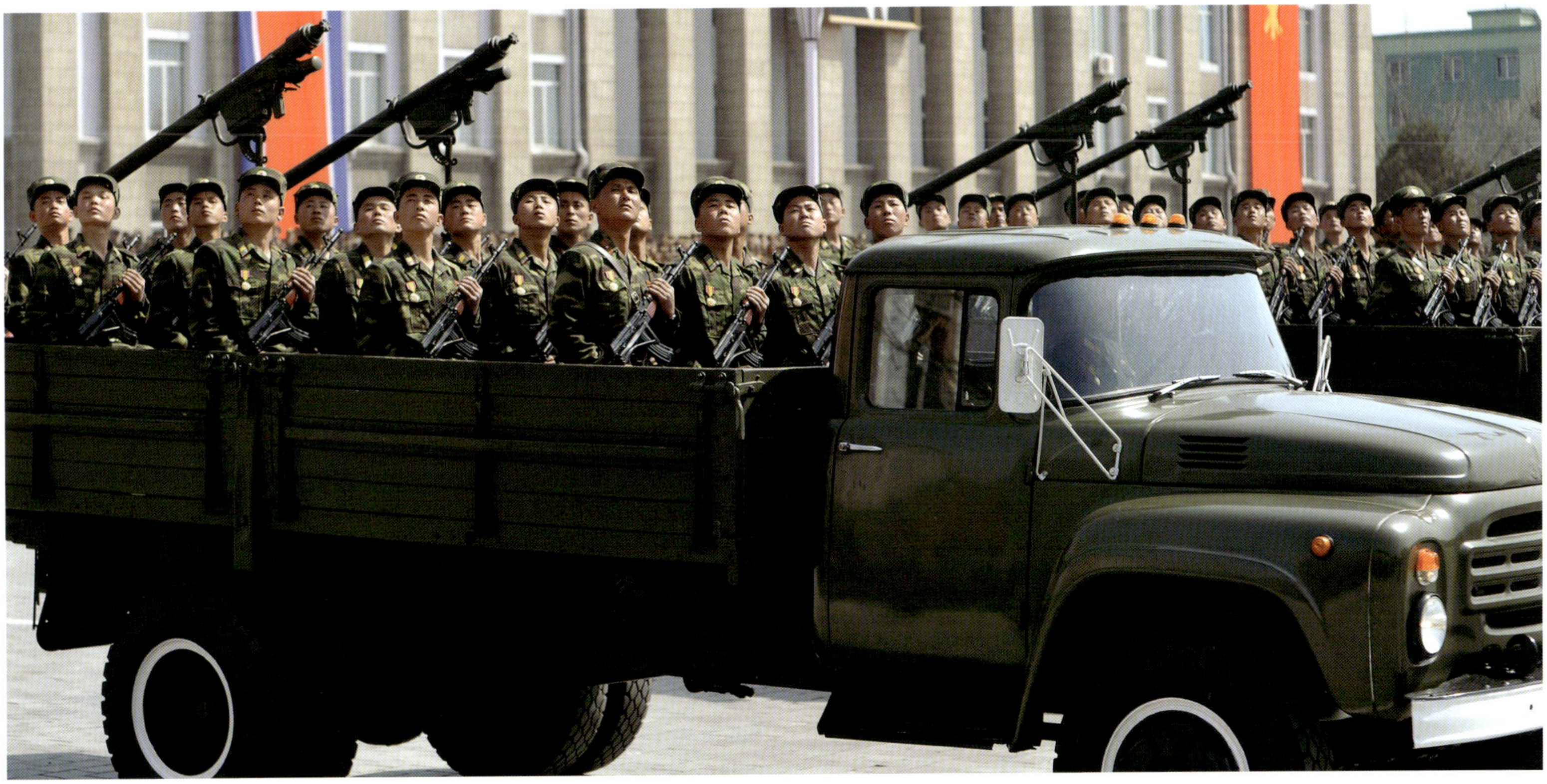

▲ Mobile missile launchers 이동식 미사일 발사기

▼ Artillery 포병대

Antiaircraft systems
대공 시스템

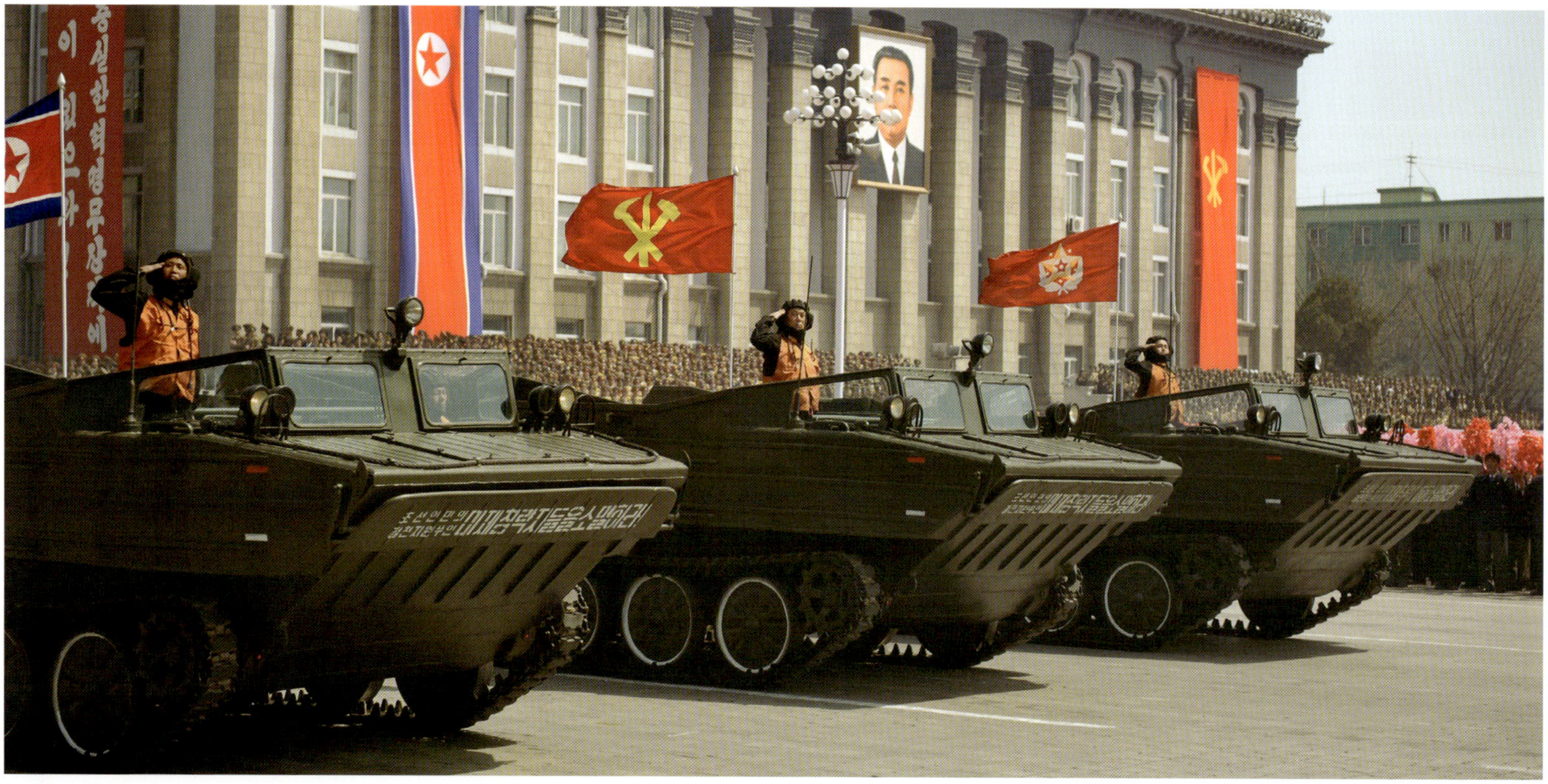

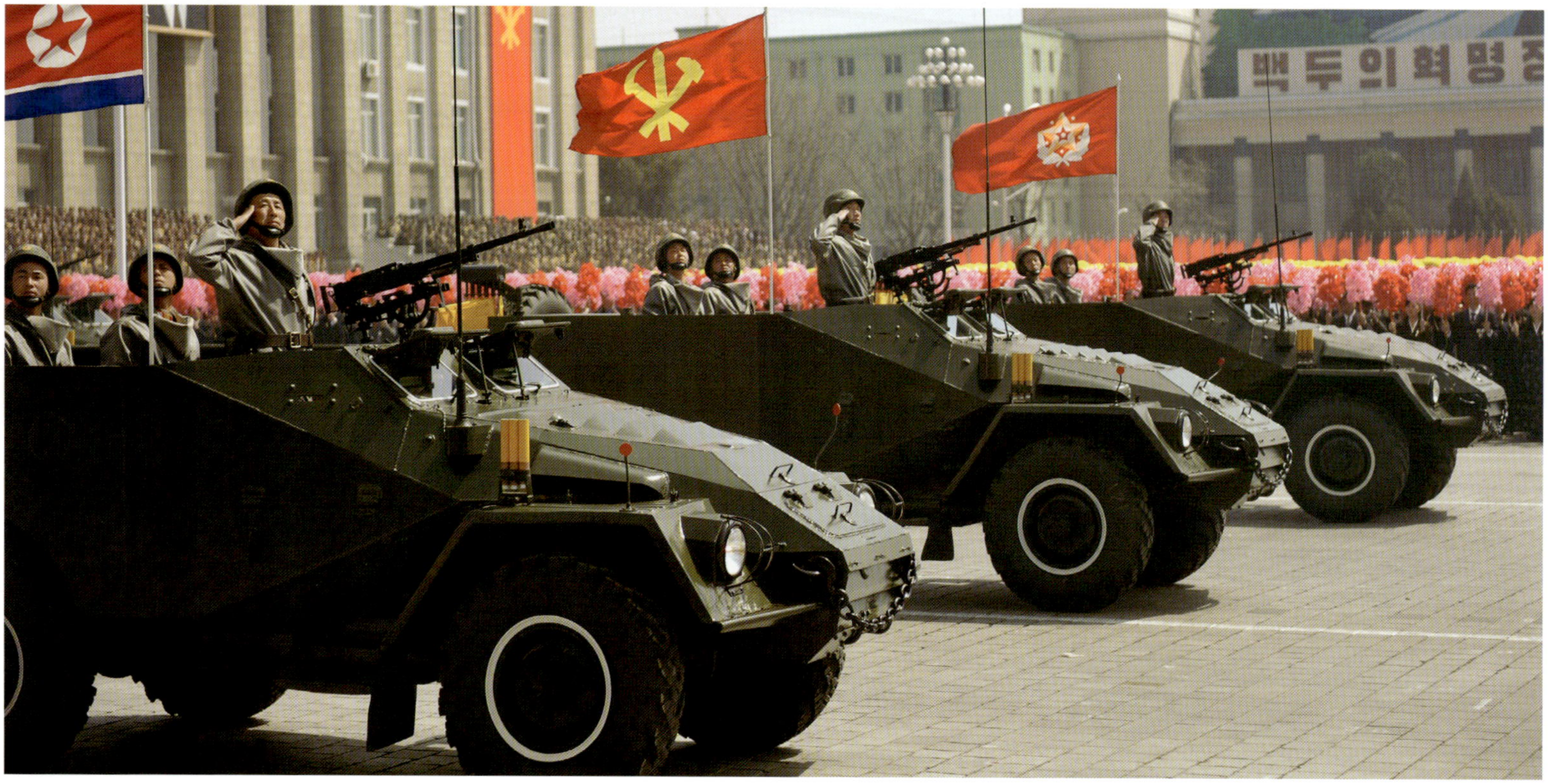
백두의혁명정

▲ ▼ ◄ ▶

Armored vehicles

장갑차량들

▲▼▶
Mobile Missile Launchers
이동식 미사일 발사대

126

▲ Rudimentary North Korean drones 초보적 수준의 북한 드론

▲▼ Rocket launchers 로켓 발사기

People holding plastic flower bouquets ▶
gathered in front of the grandstand
인조 꽃다발을 들고 주석단 앞에 모인 사람들

▲ North Korean troops 북한 군대

▲▼ MIG 29 aircraft overflying downtown Pyongyang 평양 시내를 날고 있는 MIG 29 전투기

▲▼ People waving plastic flower bouquets in front of the grandstand of Kim Jong-un 김정은이 있는 주석단 앞에서 인조 꽃다발을 흔들고 있는 사람들

131

Kim Jong-un applauding the crowd at the end of the military parade
열병식이 끝난 후 군중들에게 박수를 보내는 김정은

▲ Kim Jong-un waving to the crowd at the end of the military parade 열병식이 끝난 후 군중들에게 손을 흔드는 김정은

◄
The Fox News broadcasting team while interviewing a participant under the strict surveillance of a North Korean guide
북한 가이드의 엄중한 감시 속에서도 참가자와 인터뷰를 하고 있는 폭스 뉴스 방송국 팀

▲ The famous Juche Tower 유명한 주체탑
▼ Fireworks celebrating the 100th anniversary of the birth of Kim Il-sung 김일성 탄생 100주년을 기념하는 불꽃놀이

▲ Grand finale of fireworks celebrating the 100th anniversary of the birth of Kim Il-sung
김일성 탄생 100주년 기념 행사의 마지막을 장식하는 불꽃놀이

▶ Fireworks at the Juche Tower
주체탑 주변을 수놓는 불꽃놀이

◀
North Koreans applauding while watching the fireworks
불꽃놀이를 지켜보며 박수를 치고 있는 북한 사람들

136

▲ Musical concert celebrating the 100th anniversary of the birth of Kim Il-sung
김일성 탄생 100주년을 기념하는 음악 공연

◀ North Koreans watching the fireworks
불꽃놀이를 구경하는 북한 사람들

Synchronized dances and fireworks celebrating the 100th anniversary of the birth of Kim Il-sung

김일성 탄생 100주년을 기념하는 단체 무용과 불꽃놀이